ZIG AND ZAG

IN

Strawberry Jelly

Town House Dublin

Why Rhinoceroses don't swim in the sea!
- a wowsville poem by Zig.

i

I have a rhino buddy called Bjorn,
who lives near a bicycle shop in a place called Westmorn.
Last Tuesday I asked him, ever so politely
"Bjorn, why don't Rhinos swim in the sea?"

ii

The reason" he said "I want to make quite clear;
it's the price of an Ice cream...it's just too dear,
not to mention the sand wedged between my toes
or that awful pink candyfloss getting stuck up my nose
It makes a right mess, but not only that -
ever tried to find a Rhino-sized kiss-me-quick hat!"

iii

"Bjorn," I said "Those reasons can't be.
Why on earth don't you swim in the sea?"
Bjorn replied, "I guess I'll have to come clean,
It's just that ocean swimming isn't my scene!"

DUSTIN'S BUILDERS LTD. (½ the job in twice the time!) THE JOB

What you need: 17" x 3" quarter mullet beams, a bit of bracing, a ton of nails, The Clancey brothers — Hughie and his brother Hughie, a few cups of tea, some stale bikkies, a bit of chat and a good reason why you can't start the job 'til next Tuesday. The real price X 3.

1. MOVE IN THE JCBS TO DIG A HOLE
2. TEA BREAK
3. PUT UP THE SCAFFOLDING
4. TEA BREAK
5. DRILL A FEW HOLES

6. THE BUILDERS HOLIDAY FORTNIGHT

Dear Missus,
Took the Hi-ace down the long mile road and headed west with Hughie's tent.
Your only man,
Dustin. HUGHIE. X

MISSUS
THE JOB

7. CHUCK IN A FEW RAWL PLUGS AND IT'S A JOB WELL DONE

4x4

8. TEA BREAK

9. HERE'S YOUR BILL, MISSUS

BILL

BUT ALL I WANTED WAS A SHELF !!

JUST WHEN YOU THOUGHT IT WAS SAFE TO GO BACK
INTO THE OCEAN !

THE GOOD
The Bad
and the
WOBBLY

JOIN CAP'N U-BOAT AND SNORKELMAN IN A
SUPERSONIC, SENSATIONAL, SUB-AQUA
ADVENTURE .

Arooooooah, read on super-hero fans !!

IT WAS A BEAUTIFUL SUNNY DAY AT THE BEACH. CHILDREN RAN AROUND WITH ICE-CREAM IN THEIR HANDS, MOTHERS AND FATHERS LAY AROUND WITH SUN CREAM ON THEIR BELLIES.

BUT SOMETHING STRANGE WAS ABOUT TO HAPPEN. WITHOUT WARNING
THERE WAS A GIANT 'WOBBLY' NOISE, AND WHERE MOMENTS BEFORE
THERE WERE WAVES OF DEEP BLUE SEA, THERE WERE NOW RIPPLES
OF RED STRAWBERRY JELLY.

WHAT A MESS GANG! IF THAT FAMILY OF YIKY GLOBS REACH THE SEASIDE, YOU MIGHT AS WELL SELL YOUR SURFBOARDS AND PACK UP YOUR PICNICS. THIS WAS A STRAWBERRY ALERT, ONE WORSE THAN A RED ALERT.

WHAT WE NEED NOW IS A SUPERHERO TO SAVE THE DAY!

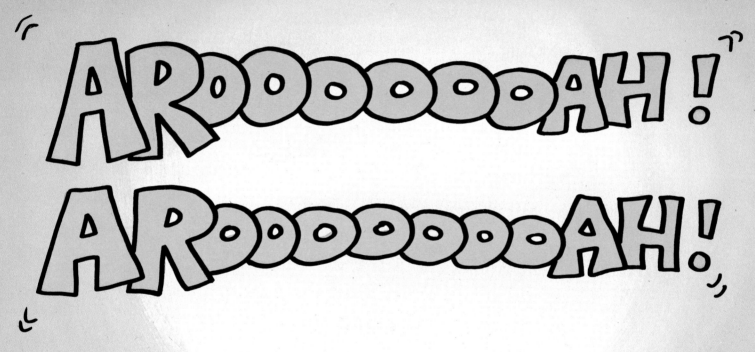

AROOOOOOAH!

AROOOOOOOAH!

IS IT A BIRD? IS IT A PLANE? IS IT A WHALE BURPING?

NO.. IT'S CAPTAIN U-BOAT, SUB-AQUATIC SUPERHERO AND PERSONAL FRIEND OF JACQUES CUSTARD, WITH HIS FAITHFUL SIDE KICK, SNORKELMAN!
AROOOOOOOOAH!
U BOAT

A FEW AQUAMINUTES LATER THE AQUAMOBILE TOUCHED DOWN IN A DUSTY DESERT TOWN. OUR DYNAMIC DRIPS DISEMBARKED IN DISGUISE AND DISAPPEARED INTO THE DESERTED DOWNTOWN.

"OH BOY, WHAT A BEAUTIFUL PLACE TO GO FOR A SWIM" SAID CAP'N U-BOAT.
"WHAT?" QUESTIONED A PUZZLED SNORKELMAN, "CAP'N HAVE YOU GONE MAD? THERE'S NO WATER IN SIGHT!"
CAP'N U-BOAT GRABBED SNORKY, "TRUST ME SNORKY, IT'S MY FLAN.. I MEAN PLAN, YOU PUDDING!!"
"OH IT'S A PLAN!" (he's a bit slow!)

A PAIR OF SNEAKY EYES FOLLOWED THE DRIPPY DUO AS THEY WALKED THROUGH THE TOWN. SUDDENLY CAP'N U-BOAT STARTED TO BLOW UP HIS ARMBANDS. "WOW, THIS LOOKS LIKE A GREAT POOL. I CAN'T WAIT TO DIVE IN AND SPLASH AROUND."
THERE WAS A PAUSE ...... THEN SNORKELMAN MUMBLED "OH YEAH I CAN'T WAIT TO DIVE IN." (He's very slow!)

SNORKY AND U-BOAT DIVED IN. THEY SPLASHED ABOUT IN THE SAND.
"LOOK AT ME CAP'N" SAID SNORKELMAN "I'M DOING THE ZOGGY-
PADDLE". SUDDENLY A STRANGE FIGURE APPEARED AND STARTED
SCREAMING "THERE'S NO WATER HERE, THERE'S NO HORRIBLE WATER.
I HATE WATER, STOP SPLASHING IN MY BEAUTIFUL DRY SAND!"

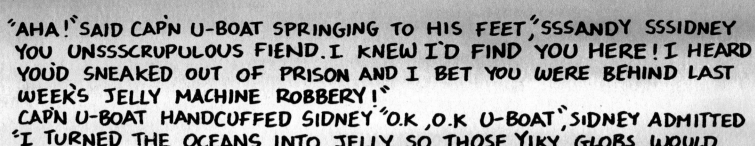

"AHA!" SAID CAP'N U-BOAT SPRINGING TO HIS FEET, "SSSANDY SSSIDNEY YOU UNSSSCRUPULOUS FIEND. I KNEW I'D FIND YOU HERE! I HEARD YOU'D SNEAKED OUT OF PRISON AND I BET YOU WERE BEHIND LAST WEEK'S JELLY MACHINE ROBBERY!"

CAP'N U-BOAT HANDCUFFED SIDNEY "O.K, O.K U-BOAT", SIDNEY ADMITTED "I TURNED THE OCEANS INTO JELLY SO THOSE YIKY GLOBS WOULD RID THE EARTH OF ALL ITS HORRIBLE WATER. BOY, I HATE WATER!"

MEANWHILE SNORKELMAN WAS STILL SWIMMING IN THE SAND (he's a bit...well, y'know!)

THE AQUAMOBILE TOOK OFF AS SNORKELMAN WEIGHED THE ANCHOR. THEY U-TURNED TOWARDS THE BEACH AND CAP'N U-BOAT BUSILY WORKED ON AN ANTI-JELLY REMEDY...TIME WAS RUNNING OUT!

JUST AS THEY ARRIVED THE YIKY GLOB FAMILY WERE RENTING OUT
THEIR DECK CHAIRS. CAP'N U-BOAT AND SNORKY DASHED TO THE
SHORE, THEY HAD TO BE QUICK. IF THE YIKY GLOBS NOTICED THE
JELLIED OCEAN, IT WOULD BE A DISASTER.

OUR HERO IN BLUE WAS AS QUICK AS LIGHTNING AND SHOT HIS HARPOON-O-LASER WHICH WAS FULL OF ANTI-JELLY REMEDY INTO THE SEA. WITHIN SECONDS THE OCEAN WAS ONCE MORE A FAMILIAR DEEP BLUE.
CAP'N U-BOAT HAD SAVED THE DAY...WHAT A GUY!!

AS THEY WERE LEAVING THE BEACH TO BRING SIDNEY BACK TO JAIL SNORKELMAN ASKED THE FAMILY OF YIKY GLOBS (who hadn't noticed any of the commotion) WOULD THEY LIKE A BOWL OF JELLY.

MR YIKY GLOB TURNED TO SNORKELMAN AND REPLIED, "NO THANKS, WE'RE ALL ON A **DIET**! BUT I WOULDN'T SAY NO TO A BIG GLASS OF **WATER** !!"
UH-OH, SNORKY GOT THAT SINKING FEELING AGAIN.

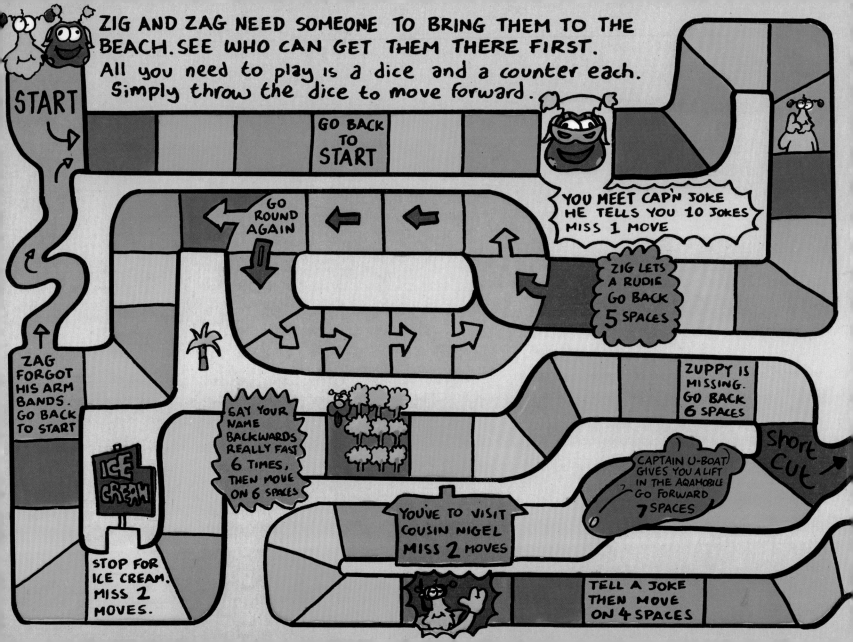

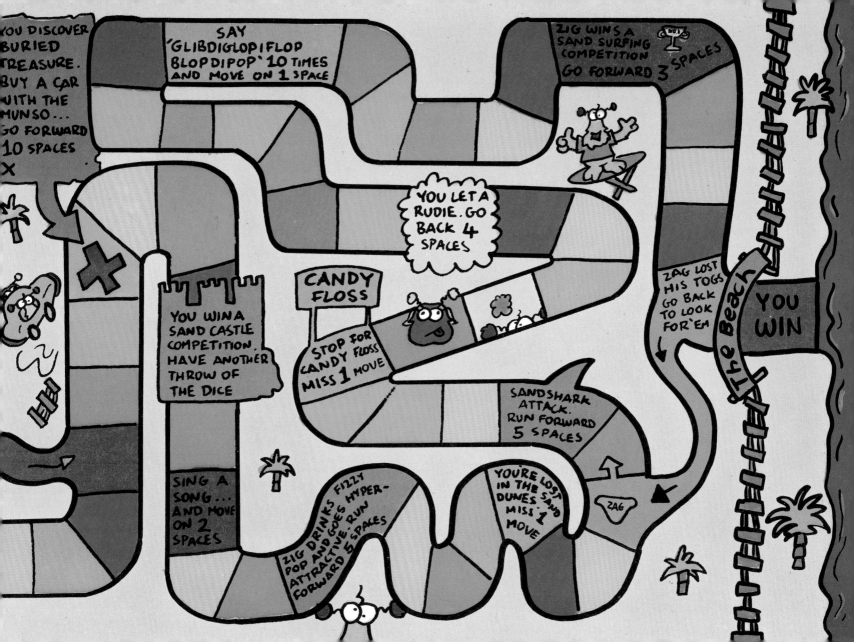

One summer, many years ago Zag and I went on our holidays to a place called Spooksville. Why Spooksville? Well, Zag booked the tickets and we all know he's not so hot when it comes to reading... he thought it was a place where they drink soup all the time!

As soon as we arrived at the hotel I began to worry. It was an old broken-down castle covered in cobwebs. The hotel manager was a strange creepy man with a hump (that was the name of his pet camel!) Things were looking rather spooky.

We asked the manager what room we were staying in and he said "Yoor in dee blessst loom in dee glottel". Then he put in his teeth and started again "You're in the best room in the hotel." Just as he said this, there was a loud clap of thunder which meant either Zag had let a rudie or some spooky things were in our room!

"Follow me to your room, sirs!" cackled the ugly manager. We all set off up the old rickity staircase. All of a sudden Zag screamed. "Arrrrrrgh!" he yelled (cause that's how you write screams in cartoons.) "What happened Zag?" I asked "Did you see a ghost or maybe a headless horseman?" He was shaking "No, you stood on my foot buster!"

After a few hours we got to the 13th floor. We asked the manager what room we were in, and he said room 13. There was another clap of thunder, which meant Zag shouldn't have eaten twenty-five packets of baked bean and curry crisps or that something really spooky was lurking in our room... for once I hoped it was Zag!

We walked into our room, we were both shaking (the heating wasn't on!) Then I really started to get scared; we were on the 13th floor in room 13, and right in front of us was the most hideous thing we had ever seen...

... green and orange paisley-coloured wallpaper! We're talking gross-out factor 9. We both sat on the bed to recover from the shock when Zag said something rather strange; "You're not scared, Zig? I mean, it's only an old myth about the haunted wardrobe in room 13 on the 13th floor!" "The what?" I stuttered.

Zag then told me that the wardrobe in our room had been haunted for many, many years by a horrible blue ghosty from beyond the twilight zone!
Uh-oh, I thought, now that is scary, very scary!!

All of a sudden the wardrobe started to move. It was shaking back and forth. I was shaking too, but Zag remained cool, as ever. Instead of being a complete scaredy sissy he bravely announced, "Don't worry Zig, I'll open it up and confront this blue ghosty once and for all!"

Zag walked slowly towards the wardrobe and creaked open the rusty old hinged door. I could hardly bear to watch; would there be a ghastly blue ghost from beyond the twilight zone lurking inside? And would it gobble up my poor brave spotty brother?
As the door opened, out jumped...

Yes, it was Zuppy! Zag, Zuppy and the ugly hotel manager had played a trick on me..ha! ha! very funny, but of course, I knew it was them all along and I was only pretending to be scared. As it turned out we were in Soupsville after all, and we whiled away the hours dining on banana and grape, mustard and apple, strawberry and gravy soup for the rest of our holiday. Boy, we had a fabaroony time!

MY HOLIDAY DIARY by Cousin Nigel

boring

MONDAY
If Monday was a smell it would smell worse than Zag's socks! Uncle Fred, my stupid dad brought me to a stupid caravan park beside the stupid sea. Ive been here five minutes and Im bored already. Holidays are for stupid people. I want to go home... even though I hate being at home Im bored, bored, bored.

TUESDAY
I was forced to go fishing with dad today. Theres only one thing more stupid than my cousin Zig and thats a fish.. although a fish is better looking and not half as smelly. Anything that eats worms must be extra-thick and needs a good thumping. Im so bored I could blow my nose into one of Zag's sandwiches! bored, bored bored!

CAP'N Jokes — Joke PAGE

What do you call a fly without wings?
A walk.

WHAT CAN FLY UNDER WATER?
A bee in a submarine.

What's black and white with red spots?
Ted with measles

WHAT IS RHUBARB?
Embarrassed celery

WHAT HAS A BOTTOM AT ITS TOP?
A Leg

What has knobs and wobbles?
Jellyvision

What illness do chickens suffer from?
People pox

How do you keep flies out of the kitchen? Put a bucket of manure in the living room.

WHAT'S THE DIFFERENCE BETWEEN TAPIOCA AND FROGSPAWN? Not a lot.

WHY DID THE APPLE CRUMBLE?
Because the banana split

What do you call five bottles of Lemonade? A POP GROUP

WHY DID THE SPACEMAN WALK? 'cause he'd missed the bus.

What's yellow and smells of bananas? MONKEY SICK

ZIG: My cousin does bird impressions.
ZAG: Does he sing?
ZIG: No, he eats worms.

OULD YOU BE A NINJA SPACE WARRIOR FROM THE PLANET ZARKOF?

It's not as easy as you might think, buster. If you can answer these six questions you could become a Ninja Space warrior!

1. WHAT WOULD YOU USE TO DEFEND YOURSELF AGAINST A GORKLE FROM THE PLANET FORKLE?
Ⓐ A FRYING PAN   Ⓑ A DYNO-BLASTER SHIELD
Ⓒ A CHIP PAN   Ⓓ A HEAD OF CABBAGE

2. HOW DO YOU GREET ANOTHER NINJA WARRIOR?
Ⓐ HELLO   Ⓑ GOODBYE   Ⓒ DANDRUFF   Ⓓ パミ1ン'ウド

3. FOUR BROWN FLODGES HAVE YOU SURROUNDED. WHAT DO YOU DO?
Ⓐ SING THE NINJA WARRIOR SONG   Ⓑ EAT THEM.
Ⓒ SHOUT "YABBA HOOLABULA"
Ⓓ BLAST THEM WITH YOUR ZERON SWORD.

4. HOW MANY NINJA WARRIORS CAN YOU FIT IN A MINI?
Ⓐ 48,000   Ⓑ 4   Ⓒ NONE   Ⓓ POLYUNSATURATED MARGARINE

5. PRINCESS GLURK IS IN DISTRESS. WHAT DO YOU DO?
Ⓐ USE ALL YOUR NINJA POWERS TO SAVE HER
Ⓑ CALL THE FIRE BRIGADE
Ⓒ POLYUNSATURATED MARGARINE
Ⓓ TELL HER TO GET OUT OF DISTRESS AND WEAR ANOTHER DRESS INSTEAD

6. IN AN EMERGENCY, WHAT FORM OF TRANSPORT SHOULD A NINJA WARRIOR NEVER TAKE TO GET TO A FAR OFF GALAXY?
Ⓐ A NINJA SPACE WARRIOR CRAFT CM 4.
Ⓑ ROCKET BOOSTER MOH 5
Ⓒ A POGO STICK   Ⓓ THE BUS.

ANSWERS
1. Ⓓ All Gorkles hate cabbage. 2. Ⓐ Of course, silly.
3. Ⓑ Brown Flodges are the No.1 tastiest chocolate bars in the galaxy.
4. Ⓒ The elephants wouldn't get out.
5. Ⓑ 'cause Princess Glurk has a habit of giving you big sloppy kisses when she's rescued...yuk!
6. Ⓓ There are no pockets in a Ninja warriors uniform...where would you keep your bus fare?